Liquorice.

Written by:

Bernie-the-Bolt.

Greetings

Hello and welcome to the first edition of 33 punchy, non-fiction poems. Packed with more punches than ***'Punch & Judy'***, you're in for a real treat. Enjoy.

Please be aware that the content in this book contains language which some readers may on occasion, find offensive.

Dedication.

This book is dedicated to my supportive family who I love very dearly - especially my amazing sister, my lovely friend 'Maid Marian' and our Roadie Paul and also my new-found friend - The Gingerbread Man.

Thank you for all your support and immense encouragement on my journey so far and thank you for believing in me and supporting my passion, which I thoroughly enjoy.

I'd also like to thank Eileen, a former childhood Social Worker - now close friend, who has been a major influence in my life. She is an amazing woman and an incredible role model. She's that cool that even Dexy who goes running at midnight knows her. Groovy eh?

I could not have done this without your input. You all make the world a better place with your infectious spirits, knowledge, friendship, love; positivity and laughter.

All royalties will be donated to the Terrence Higgins Trust, which works to educate and support people diagnosed and living with HIV/AIDS in the UK.

CONTENTS

About the Author.

Bernadette O'Horo was born in Yorkshire. She shares her life with friends and family and has a keen interest in linguistic anthropology, psychology, music and photography.

Her musical influences range from Duran Duran, Adam and the Ants, Billy Idol, Madness and Culture Club; to the one and only revolutionary Punk Band - The Clash.

Places of escape include St. Ives and Bolton Abbey and her favourite Superhero is Banana Man. Why, you ask? Because Yellow is a warm colour and the world needs more Magic.

Quotes created and written by the Bolt:

"Although bitten by a Crocodile, we'll always be raised by the Sun".

"Keep company good and keep good company".

"Although extremely vulnerable, ever brave must we always be".

"Birds that sit, fish and Birds that fish, share".

"Carve with Gold. Not with Wood".

"Smoke with Ink, to create a new Drink".

"In a world full of Jokers, be a Penguin".

"Less Love of Power and more Power of Love. Less Liquorice Footprints and more pleasantries, like a Dove".

Political Poems
Liquorice Footprints.

Yes. Capitalism is failing people!
Hungry mouths, fragile bones.
Government's sucking: 'Ice-Cream Cones'.

Categorization to determine eligibility.
Welcome to the contested invisibility
***Liquorice Language** on: 'Thorny Crowns'.*

Democracy rises like Bread, in all towns
Smokes my pockets, leaves me in slums.
Paints me in numbers, with filthy bums

Spaghetti Junction, as we lose control.
Diced like meat, cubed into their hole
I'm ejecting cookies, rolled up to throw.

Into your hands, as you chalk us; down low
Self-Assessment Forms, in a pickled mess.
Under pressure, intense feelings of stress

'I Daniel Blake' deserved better, a fair trial.
Unjust actions left me 'Out Cold'; in style
I'll just lick the gutter and die with a disease.

Spit-Polish your shoes. Bent down, on my knees.
*It's time to get **'Anarchic'** and fight back hard*
*With **'Punk Fashion Nails'**, for many blow; scarred.*

Let's turn back in time, 'Cher'; 50 years on the clock
*To relive those conditions, engulfed in: **'Black Rock'.***
Exploitative Banners, that's where Demons; are used

With glass shots that scorn the innocent, fully bruised.
Beggars can be choosers and sit drowning, in blood
*Frying the hopes of the: **'Deserving',** in sweaty mud.*

Diamond tears in my mind, machete knife in my heart.
*Drinking **red-liquid** tears the flesh: "It's dead smart".*
Dominelli States: "We need optimistic measures".

"To end marginalization and calm, stormy weathers".
Get on this train and look me, deep in the eyes:
Don't you dare tell me, you can't hear; broken cries.

A fine-tuned machine, 'Turing' with: Golden Clogs.
Wanna sing with the Elite? Or swim with the Frogs?
'Mr. Monopoly's Board' continues, this brutal game

Swaying with 'Skin Heads', injecting stigmas and shame.
It's Paper to the Gods, we're like ghosts of the night
Enigmatic Strangers filling, 'Common Benches'; to bite.

Controversial ideals stamp veins, to create a Cold War
*Logged by a: **'Callous Fascist',** who is thirsty for more.*
'Scatmen' eat the cherries, freshly laced for tomorrow

Square slates in the grass, 'Whisper Careless'; in sorrow.
Corporate Dinosaurs lurking, the hall of Good Wealth:
"How's it hanging Street Kidz? All Mental, in Health?".

Lobotomized in a queue under, the: 'Rabbit Proof Fence'.
Leather Brained, Chelsie Smiles; to keep up the pretense
'Left-Wing Functionalism' - 'Marx', envelopes at the seals.

Feminists dance to the beat, sexes' back in slick heels!
'Right-Wingers' on the pitch, a poor match is played
'Thatcher's' pulling strings, dressed in Marmalade.

'Guy's' plotting with 'Marc', behind 'Almond' Sun-glasses.
Privatization on the Markets, dominating: World Classes
Lipstick on your collars or bags of sand? It's your choice.

Those Yellow helpers are swallowed, to needle your voice.
'Billy, He Bragg's', sat on 'Changeling's Ward'; Psychiatric
What's the next move? A bloody clone? Get in: 'Hat-trick'.

Lemon Zest spikes your platter with juices, bittersweet.
Bewildered Cattle, ruffle feathers; to stick to his feet
Smooth Russian Criminals, deep-throat in Orange Salt.

Angelina's not here. Shit! Well, let's ask... Usain Bolt.
Skeletons' rock in the dust, as the clouds light up grey
Concentration Camp is out. It's now Holocaust Day.

Penned with Illuminous Ink, for: 'Ian's Dury', it calls.
We're just like **'Pink Floyd',** dirty bricks in the walls
Human Rights, in a skip. Dynamite bombs, the tank.

'Michael's got his Caine'. Can't escape, a good spank!
Minsky told of a genetic weakness, unstable in tune
Whilst Mr. Apples blows out, the candle-lit room.

Unemployment high rise, drizzled; in puddles of Honey.
'Voldemort's' on your back, boiling you like: 'Bugs Bunny'
Pollution choking tongues, with glitter kisses of Silk.

As you sit sipping on wooden straws, curdled in Milk
Fine Brown Sugar, which Crystallizes: 'Political Winks'.
Normalization on tap, like Pepper Whiskey; one drinks

'Power Rangers' mogadon, by suede booting; with a tick.
It's a 'Rat Race' fully stemmed, by a: 'Colourful Prick'.

<u>ODE to the Bourgeoisie.</u>

<u>We are all Daniel Blake.</u>

Facing 'Injustice' and filling out forms
To meet ideologies and expected norms.
Proving our worth, by living in squalor
Tied to the Bourgeoisies', Dog Collar.

*Marking in **Purple**. But thinking in **Red**.*
Seven days a week. Peanut Butter is spread.
The Bent and the Shady, leave us fully bruised
Yet, for some the system; goes on getting used.

Nobody listens. We're marked down on White.
*And we can't even afford, just; **1** bottle of Sprite*
We're skint & demoralized, for we drown in thick blood.
As this system starves people, with: 'Hot Toasted Mud'.

***'Marxism'** is a belter that **'Park Life'**, powerfully portrays*
Epitomizing how those in need, are stabbed in many ways.
Eating raw food out of cans, can't afford clothes for our own
No hot water, a lack of sanity; selling our souls to the unknown.

Kids they're getting bullied and suicide, to: 'Paradise City'; it calls
*As we're wedged into the cracks of: **'Pink Floyd's'**, feculent walls.*
A lack of education and single mums, that are off: 'Trainspotting'
Tarmac lungs they multiply, like fresh cream; in Cornwall, clotting.

Living in Slums, infested and Human Rights, that chalk the veins
'Sexualized Traffic' for profit, piping people; into icy bags that stains.
Social Security? Dear Darlings. Don't be daft, we're going, right down
As the places where we live, are like 'Psycho Bob'; in a ligneous crown.

Loneliness and degradation, people licking the gutters; to find a friend
But for some, it's bloody carnage; as 'Deathly Hallows', bell their end.
Some of us are demonized by the media, who wear tight leather vests
Sugar coating papers in candy floss, with glitter bullets in our chests.

Living off £50 a week, to provide all the necessities; that you so need
For your family who are desperate, to kiss goodbye to: Sour Aniseed.
'Political Riots' of fury we spark, hoping to change the: 'Groovy Gang'.
That's run by a set of: Theoretical Badgers, driving a: Volcanic Bang.

'Institutional Barbarity' against vulnerable people, who pay their dues
'White Dee Benefits' by taking the piss, as our dignity we do; but lose.
We are Citizens. We are Human. Not Random Numbers. *Can't you see?*
What your 'Bread Winning Tactics', are doing to yourself and to me.

We are all just 'Nymphs & Thugs', getting laid by: 'Willow's Eerie Creek'.
Sucked like Liquorice and bathed in spit; for 'Poverty' paints, us bleak.
Drinking from 'Nickelback's Bottle', to numb the pain; that rings our ears.
'Scarlett Pimpernel' is on the rise, drowning us in stained glass; velvet tears.

We've got misogyny and gender inequality. Shame on these goats, who talk.
Gnawing down on a crimson tranquillizer, for Aristocracy drips in our walk.
Stuck to the same brown bristled brush, that's basked in five spices; sweet
We tap to the: 'Slavers Illegal Remedies', superglued underneath our feet.

We've got oil rigs on our thighs and attitudes, like full bearded chickens' jerk
It's a dance of a thousand losers all fighting for jobs, for they need the work.
We can make sure that 'Cathy Comes Home'. So that ***Rainbows*** *shine, like Silk.*
And change the desserts that are offered in mugs, with: Cheesy Straws, to Milk.

An Egg and Spoon Race sweeps this Nation; to run wildly like: 'Fatboy Slim'.
Busting a gut and sinking in sand. To rock with the: Horses and their Spicy Gin.
Pedophiles 'Forty Lickin' online and the 'Guvnors' say to rehab, no metal bars
Digestive crumble rattles our bones. Chain them to the seats of: 'Numan's Cars'.

Some of us come from: 'St. Trinians', but our 'Biscuits'; are now being cut in half
Services that are vital to 'Penny's Arcade'. Yet, we hang high like slaughtered calf.
Taxmen smoke our pockets, like Fagan. To pay for the rebuild of: Crystal Palace.
Fingers twist on 'Monopoly's Board'; as they serve: 'Pink Pleonexia' & 'Malice'.

Female Genital Mutilation, innocent flesh it gets hacked; like computer screens
Sadistic Egos dance in cloudy lemonade, lighting up: 'Danger Mouse Machines'.
Polishing 'Adam Ant Burkas', boxing matches; where culture takes, full control
A landmark court case to wear our Crosses. As the 'Black & White' dices; do roll.

Pin Stripe *Religion carves* ***bold*** *letters, into those people who are: 'Gay and Proud'.*
Buzzcock the ward for 'Straitjackets & Plugs', to cure: 'Satan's Horny Bone Crowd'.
Humiliated if you don't look like sassy models, who own the covers of: Glossy Porn.
Segregated and Stigmatized as delinquents and stuffed in: 'Yellow, Salty Pop-Corn'.

Words can paint a million pictures, but none can compare to this catastrophic tale.
For Robots pipe the puppet strings, as they peg the: 'Tangy Fish' online, for sale.

Like Bread. We Rise.

Yes. Down in the bottom, of a: Deep, Dark Hole
Inequality rises like burning fires in: Charcoal.
Ridiculed by the men, who wore leather pants:
"You're a: Scullery Maid! Flee ridden in Antz".

Bashed into biscuits, by the beastly who ruled
C'mon let's march for our rights, to be fueled.
A loss of social structure? Get stuffed! Fat Clown.
For when we win the War. You'll be licking, our Crown.

Smashing windows with bricks, butterflies in our pit
Marginalized by Oppression and sunk deep; boiling in spit.
With a flame in our bellies, we skim the streets to protest:
Dandy clippers we use, to curl the hairs on your chest!

We are the Suffragettes. The Soldiers. Preparing for battle
With glitter bullets and loud voices, no sheep; just raw cattle.
Riots with the Police, playing: 'Punch & Judy', with our flesh.
Feeling worthless and cold blooded; like dead chickens' in mesh.

But still, we shall rise like 'Maya Angelou', once sweetly wrote:
Dancing with diamonds on our thighs, to get the women's vote.
Treated like fish to be eaten, on the males' platter; laced in salt:
Crystal tears they sting our eyes, locked into: 'Krueger's Vault'.

Separated from our children and treated like prisoners: 'Sick'.
Needled by a filthy system, that's 'Kester'; 'Rae Earls' - Mental Tick.
Smoking buildings like chalk, because the men won't hear us speak:
"I'd give up now if I were you, women are like runny soup; too weak".

But, John Stuart Mill puckered up; with glossy lips, he rallied round
In favour of Harriet Taylor, who Fox-Trot quick; on Peachy ground.
Look at what we've faced! The Platinum Clock it chimed, hard beat
With Pebbled Stones and Scarlett Thorns, engraved into our feet.

The inferiority of women is hideous, it was all a lie enforced by law
Dipped in 'Renton's Fizzy Pop' and dry roasted by: KP's knobbly paw.
Purple, White and Green, press down on these spikes of: Sex Appeal:
'Injustice Buckets' we fill to 'Hyacinth', Bright Oranges'; Shady Deal.

Social Reforms for Unity, to wet drench the land in Milk and Honey:
Kiss goodbye to Carcass Crunch, who boiled you like: 'Bugs Bunny'.
If in this modern world, you are not even: 'Political Crows'; who care
Dear 'Rapunzel's', please think before you mark, your paper; with a flare.

Think of the polluted shoes, that walked into: 'Herod's', Bruised Rain
Carrying 'Gossips' Heavy Wooden Cross, nailed with pellets of pain.
Metal Diggers they peck my head, Jack knifing me like: Tuna Chunks.
To move in Marillion's, Clash of: 'Jigsaws', breeding with the PUNKS!

*Media, it twisted the papers, to **'Paint us Black';** like 'Jagger' - Rolling*
Ten 'Pins' down ya 'Greasy Kings', the 21st Century is: Skillfully Bowling.
'Death like the Hallows' interwoven, with 'Timmins' Five Big Giant Sins
Cutting back to Epson Derby 1913, taken out ransomed; on all 4 limbs.

*1928 saw us sticking stamps like lollipops, to your Jealous, **Green** Ears:*
"We fought the prejudice you threw at us and we overcame our fears".
Even though Power Tripping and Monopoly, still exists this very day
Let us remember a generation of Women, who fought for Equal Pay.

It might be criticized for being, too 'Patriarchal and Gender Biased'.
But even so, the Morris Ball goes on with: Rag 'n' Bone Messiah's.
Aniseed slips down the throats, of the Feminists here; in this room:
"Our Genitals don't define us: 'Madoons'. For we sing, in perfect tune".

Empowerment served with Salad Cream and Brandy Snap desserts
Sipping from: 'The Golden Goblet' letters, which echo: Saucy Flirts.
Blink 182 have had their day and 'Snow-White', she's still left to run
*'The Rat Race' fully stemmed in **Red,** as she remains living in; a slum.*

So, don't waste the opportunity given, to use your voice to change:
The Nut-Megs sprinkled in grit, who act like: Monkeys, ever strange
'International Women's Day', rings out, with bells on: Vintage Bikes.
Providing 'Mary Popping Pills' to twat, those: Good 'Ole Billy Sikes'.

Twisted Fingers.

*Machete Tears run **Red,** sliced in Deaths pure greed.*
*Whiskey flames cover **'Lazarus'**, in bare bones of: Aniseed*
Rustic Ashes they fall, as silence fills the broken land.
Droplets of Illuminous Ink, penetrate each withered hand

Asphyxiated in waters deep, troubled hearts will slowly heal.
Lighting up the Stadium, in Yellow forever; to conceal
Floodgates will open wide, to remember those we've lost.
Buried in an Apocalypse, of Gun-Smoke high in cost

Discrimination basked in Wine, go wash your fingers clean.
*Eat the **'Forest Fruits'** and disregard the: 'Judgement Team'.*
Lay down crystal stones and venomous weapons of decay.
*'Dallas Buying in the Club', to change the: **'Jokers Way'.***

HIV and Aids calling, is ignorance lost on: Stoney Grounds?
Contaminated needles bathed in flesh, with: 'Psychedelic Sounds'.
Unprotected Sex high-risk, destructive fires indeed; they burn
Fatal infections deep inside, flip the coins on the tables; turn.

Worldwide Politics skin tight, wrapped in: Activisms Cure.
Stepping up to tackle sub-divisions, that generations do endure
Whether innocent or unwise, don't 'Blame the Machines'; that fail.
Take Courage Thomas, Hope, seek solace; let down your veil

Pillows talk of Medication, as you label the Lepers wrist.
*Arms enclosed in **Darkness,** pocket watching the cloudy mist*
Come closer step beyond, the barriers of exclusion and pain.
*Lay down your negativity, for we are **Human as I;** the **Same.***

*Not specifically rendered **'Gay'**, for each person can fall asleep.*
Underneath the Danger Zones, where Suicide takes hold; to keep
Flatten Palms of Ice, work in conjunction upon the Battlefield.
Swipe the buttons left and take your Silver Sword and Shield

Promiscuous actions free running, injecting Drugs to spread: Disease.
Ethnic Minorities Under Surveillance, shaking Pineapples from the Trees
'Bohemian Rhapsody' in New-York, populated in Polish to Shoeshine.
'Purple Rains' in Africa, educating the Dragons to chase the line

*Taste the **Skittled Rainbow**, soaked in solid Gold; ever sweet.*
***Red Ribbons** of Silk to commemorate, those fallen at our feet*
The 'Finest Hour' awaits, so let us salute the: 'Phoenix Call'.
Skimming tongues to cheek, as we break down: 'Berlin's Great Wall'.

Kiss the Shotgun.

They cringe at 'Five Spices' and they rock 'Heavy Fashion'
And they'll never discuss: 'Taboos' Slick Passion.
They'll hypnotize your mind and smother your bones
By incarcerating you, in rancid hail stones.

Ethnocentric; 'Miss Trunchbull' and one sided tales
Rolling you over, hay stacking; square bales.
They'll paint you as a ghost, who is off your rocker
If you don't join their candles, all you've got is beat blocker.

Controversial Ideologies imprinted, to create a Cold War.
I thought Hitler was dead? Why's he at my front door?
Stamped with Ruby letters, as they tick their Checklist.
Shouting: "This ones' a goner, for they dance with a twist".

Human Rights, I have freedom, but; they hold the pitchfork.
People's heads are messed up, dripping with powdered chalk
Paper cuts they run deep, for people's skin; it bleeds.
So, why continue to bash us like biscuits; for proceeds?

The Lambs, they called round; to spread the: 'Good Word'
But, I just stood there thinking: "What the hell? It's absurd".
All who come to the Cross, will be raised from the dead!
Anarchic fingertips, lash out: "We don't want to be fed".

I respect their views, but; it's not really for me
Because, I wear 'Baggy Trousers'; break rules and disagree.
People want life and laughter, not a game of oppression
So, pipe down and minimize; your manners of aggression.

It's up to me to challenge, in writing; this form.
Rigid thinkers who are driven by: 'Salty Pop-Corn'.
Take your Black and White Collars and the scales off your eyes.
*Donald, stop building walls and spit out those: **'Black Flies'***

Mental Health on the increase, still colouring scars
Ignorance oozing hot pants, as ***'P!nk'*** *tries the:* ***'Gay Bars'.***
Mr. Orange, his sticky liquid; is fed to the damned.
For glitter bullets in the cupboard, mark you as: 'Their Brand'.

I cannot understand what goes off, inside their bearded minds
So, I'm questioning their Ethics, by using these rhymes.
She couldn't sit in the seat, where her music; she played
As it was 'written off' and then sold to a: 'worthier, skin trade'.

Injected and abused no state of sanity, you're now cabbaged.
Do you care about the people, whose lives you've mismanaged?
I've got a torch in my hand and a sharp tongue, for dessert.
I've skimmed my tools well, to show you how to flirt!

'Careless Whispers' rattle round, as on the decks; fire plays.
Red pen, muddy stigmas; *because we don't speak: Straight A's.*
Classifications that cut-throat, costing your worth in time
You're either on 'Solid Ground' or it's Carnage. Shoes, shine.

I'd love a magic wand because, this world is cruel and it smokes
It licks candy from the gutter and sprays you with, steel oaks.
Staple, Magic Dust to your thighs and bring a can of: Graffiti
Drizzle bittersweet grammar, laced in sweat; dead meaty.

Wear your seat-belt with pride and a bullet-proof vest
Because this battle isn't over, there's more 'Acid' to digest!
Hercules frowning from the clouds; "This is not, what I meant".
"I didn't want hard hearts and prophets; monopolizing this tent".

You cannot needle bomb this generation, to think like the: 'Elite'.
Because they swipe fetching liquor and sound their own beat.
I've got dysprosium clippers in my eyes, which disfigure my flesh
And my tiny brain it's all mangled, like dead chickens'; in mesh.

I've tossed cookies in my pocket and now I'm giving them back
Because you're failing to listen and keep giving us; pure slack.
This Chronicle has left Nations, on: 'Leather Faces' - ***Death Train***
It's sad to think that 'Religious Politics', can cause so much pain!

Edwin Starr Echoes in Yellow: "Kiss, those bloody shotguns - GOODNIGHT".
And down the juices from 'Peppered Pigs', basked in sugar; as you FIGHT!

Fifty-Two Licks of: Sweet Rhythm.

When boys played the girls and girls played the boys
And 'Maggie Thatcher' ruled.
When ***'Anarchic'*** *Johnny Rotten, graced our screens*
With toxic licks, unschooled.

When Boy George laced, the papers in White
And the Clash, were strumming: 'Protest Songs'.
When Duran Duran, were challenging stereotypes
With frilly materials and fine, glittered prongs.

When unemployment, was fiercely rising
And the 'circus' stabbed us, with steely knives.
We were a generation of smoke, going up in flames
Like a ***Black Cat,*** *who had less than nine lives.*

When Television, went horribly wrong
Sparking many, controversial debates.
We were like melted butter, sinking
Between the lines, of the greasy slates.

When Oliver Reed invaded, women's space
By drinking, from the peppered bottle.
'Gender Politics', flew over the roof
Knee deep, with a powerful throttle.

When riots were fueled, by oppression
And the 1974 Miners' Strike, began.
Injustice was dripping, from salty buckets
Spewed up, from the 'Busters' - Damn!

When 'Top of the Pops', was canned
With false laughter and cheesy smiles.
Sexually exploiting, those: 'Legs & Co'.
To spice up the heartbeats, slow dials.

When Madonna was touched, for the very first time
And her image shocked, the eyes of the Nation.
This was where I, began to question my-self:
*And the concept of: '**Normalization**'.*

When Brookside aired, its first: 'Gay Kiss'
And the Church were making cakes, to cure.
'Social Construction', predesigned our life:
Unethically bashing us like biscuits, impure.

When Racism, divided our communities
And kids were caned, by 'Michael' himself.
When power imbalances, drove women to fight
For a more substantial status, of: 'Economic Wealth'.

When one, 'Flew Over the Cuckoo's Nest'
Enriching our understanding, of mental instability.
*It highlighted how, '**Collectivism** is needed'*
To plug change and accept responsibility.

When Jimmy Savile tried to fix it, for us
Then, his death brought sickening news.
We were all lining up to voice, our disgust
For this battle saw many, deeply bruise.

When 'The Pop Kidz', dominated the charts
And Vinyl records, were the 'bomb' of our days.
These are the things that tested our childhood:
Like clockwork 'turing' the clogs, of: 'Crystals, Maze'.

Anyone can be Sixth.

'Crocodile Shoes', they tap the ground.
In Candy Floss, he remains blood bound.

His face it dropped, like pebbled stones.
Thrown into high voltage, danger zones.

On vomit, he chokes; for he's got to speak.
His knees are knocking, he feels dead weak.

He stutters to the beat, for he's losing hope.
Hung dry on 'Cracklings', Duct-Tape Rope.

Whispers they dance, laced in Pungent Ale.
Egging bones sharply, with spotted Quale.

The 'Cats Eyes' linger, to exploit his worth.
"Why me?". He asks. On this God Forsaken Earth.

Marbles in his mouth, chain smoking to claw.
Like Ezekiel swinging, on a squeaky see-saw.

The Pinnacle of Distortions, control the dice.
On the 'Picket Fence', glazed in: Siberian Ice.

'Chained to a Rhythm', demanding perfection.
Humiliated & Ridiculed, by a flaky reflection.

Golf Balls lodged in a brave, intellectual soul.
He polished the exterior, of ***Black shiny coal.***

He feasted on tension, his dynamics ran wild.
A member of: 'The Smiths', outside; X-Filed.

Like a lunatic stapled, to the: 'Asylums Cell'.
Spaghetti Tears were cried at: 'Jacobs Well'.

His Skeleton rocked, into: 'Voldemort's' grave.
Flapjackin' licks of hope, to cure life's slave.

His tongue dissolves like treacle, into a can.
But the 'Pearly Gates', still chose this man.

You see, anyone can rise; to fight the fear.
If you stand with courage, upon the pier.

If you call it quits and keep running away.
*You'll never see the: **Skittled Jars,** of Clay.*

So, let's applaud the: Mashed Potato Brain.
Who Head-Shot in glass, the Nutty Grain.

In Royal Robes crowned a: Valuable King.
Pricking Veins to cause, one lethal Sting.

Justice Desserts.

Could such a Nation, live in Hate?
And fail to flip, the Gold Coined Slate?
Irrational Broadcasts, on each zone.
Cutting throats, with a brutal tone.

Hands entwined in grief skin deep.
These children should, we ever keep?
Lost in translation, 'Oh' what a mess.
Under pressure and intense stress

'Social Injustice', pained each heart.
And tore subcultures, like cattle; apart
Can we ever change moralities call?
And end the oppression, dished out to all?

Catastrophic events, upon the tracks.
Chasing pavements; to fill the cracks
Frosty stands in snow, pure white.
As those tongues, they did but; take a bite

Of Liquid Gold, dressed up in vain.
Inflicting the venom of deep, dark pain.
Smothered in Smoke, where he did lay
Amongst the rubble of: **Black Decay.**

Riddled with fear, immense pain in tow.
The 'Blasé Witness', runs way too slow.
Fractured volts in the: 'Human Eye'.
As the 'Common Law' fails; to hear our cry.

Anonymity born into 'World War One'
Bleeding us bone dry, what have you done?
Kid-Gloving Children, for their Crimes
'Slick Lawyers in Suits'; were of those times.

Drip feeding mouths, to earn a wage.
Have you forgotten the: 'Hookers' bitter rage?
Stones and bottles: the lions roared.
As a game was played on: 'Monopoly's Board'.

Mr. Apples, walks the wrong side of town.
*With **bloodstains** on his: 'Thorny Crown'*
An Ocean basked, in bittersweet tears.
With parents missing out, on precious years

Mad Hatters in the Cuckoo's Nest?
Stapling bullets of steel, into each chest.
Escaping from, the Candy Man.
Who were we to know, what they would plan?

Sleepless hours, nightmares unravel.
As in unknown hands, your son; did travel.
Little Faith in a System, walking free.
Do you even care, what they did to me?

Soft flesh vacuumed into a vault.
Through this worldly flood, high pitched in Salt.
Unconditional Love, did it fail to exist?
Cause these boys to create, a psychotic twist?

So, who are children in this place?
Just bodies that fall, far from; Sweet Grace?
"James", she cried: "I just want you back".
"Why were you the one under attack?".

"I picture your face, to have and to hold".
"For this pernicious case, has left me cold".
Papers please rearrange, your filthy tune.
From its pungent taste, of a shriveled prune.

Engraved with passion, engulfed in fire.
To adjust the 'Welfare States', flat tyre.
Souls broken by, a rusty blade.
This Market knows how, to 'Skim Tight'; its trade.

Lowered down into a box, underneath the ground.
As silence remained our only sound.
Documented within the History Books.
Out of Taxpayers' Pockets, all off their hooks.

Running low on strength, as we fail to cope.
Does this mean that we, should give up hope?
Where's 'Bodie and Doyle', at this very hour?
For their practice is needed, to empower.

Chalk another side, of the Black and White Que.
To see the Lens, of: Poirot's View.
Whatever happens tomorrow, will anyone care?
Heads will keep turning, they will; but stare.

A skeletal frame broken, out in the wild.
Slave Labor to protect, the caseload of your child
Jacob did wrestle as his bones, became weak.
But 'I Daniel Blake', didn't play hide and seek.

As he drank from the cup, of a solemn mourn.
To make sure that the **Red G's Tape,** was torn.
So, take a walk with me; to remember the lost.
Burning the waves, that are uncivilized in cost!

New Blood.

Filthy fingers and Jealous hands
Invisible transactions and high demands.
Monopolizing Systems, with devious ways
New Blood for a burden, one Colour; never stays.

Intimidating Politics and Wealthy Admissions
'Paper Thin' dominated, by: Unequal Decisions.
A bloody orange aftermath and a fire, which burns
Rolled by a dense square, they all take it; in turns.

Crystal tears in the mind and disheveled looks
Pottage heads taking over, rewriting the books.
'Third World Countries' and the 'Riot Police'
'Mental Health' chained up, with no release.

Passing Batons of Steel and stamping Hearts
A faulty invention, with irregular parts.
Acidic Baths and wounded souls
Frontline Money, just hitting the goals.

A derogatory framework and categorical years
Bright Red visions, of ones' deepest fears.
Negative influences and divided ground
Hannibal Lecter; can't speak, no sound.

Catastrophic events and brittle bones
What do you make, of the unsafe zones?
An eye for an eye and a tooth for a tooth
'Pink Floyd's Education', of Bullets; Proof.

Social Injustice and Discriminatory Laws
*It's not just: **'Little Britain'**, at fault to; the cause.*
Corruption in the mix and remote controlled minds
Break down those barriers, go create some new signs.

Diversity Dances and inclusive generations
Does History account, for your conversations?
Terrorist Attacks and Cultural Wars proceeding
In Unison let's stand, to change what it's feeding.

Liquid Gold.

Bitten with one hand, then taken down; by another.
This is the very life of: 'Paper Gods', that try to smother
Asphyxiated; Oxygen lacking, the ruffled feathers; floating, round.
Freedom slowly sinking, Big Brother is watching our every sound.

False Prophets make the rules, sharp edges the colours pierce.
'Keeping up with the Appearances', wind swept by a tide, so fierce
Bittersweet tears for this existence, making it hard to peacefully swallow.
Warning Hazards to try to guess, why we are taken aboard: 'Sleepy Hollow'

'Red Hot Chili Peppers' too strong; an Apocalypse on the washing line, I see.
Crimson stained Ink running dry, all the Papers are snatched from my grasp to be
Transparent like the Rustic Ashes, will anyone confess to this Venomous Crime?
For the Centurions Clock is calling distantly, as we stand ever frozen, in time.

We forcefully bow to the **Dark Side,** *with knives wedged under our fragile skin.*
Presented with severe bruising; we are liquidized, lethargic and 'Paper Thin'.
Like a magnet pulled back and forth, we hold onto the heated wire.
With Quicksand under our feet to claim, our innocent souls; into the Raging Fire.

Can we not complain about it? Even though it is an inevitable fact to life; each day.
A 'Game of Thrones' with hungry eyes, going out of their minds; in every way
These two words sitting next to each other, are highly unusual in a daily stance.
Biting flesh to remain untouchable, whilst rocking **Tim Burton's** *- deadly glance.*

So, as we keep on bowing to the invisible; with beating hearts, forevermore.
This Paper we've worked so hard to earn, will keep shredding at our door
We the Prey will keep chasing the goal, to plan a: 'Great Escape'; going down.
But even though we try, we'll Fail; because the Golden Gods, own this town.

A Spoonful of Sugar.

Skimming those false lines, can't read about it for my eyes; they burn.
Fiddlers in another's business, they sure got lessons; they need to learn
Keep the secret, hush yourselves; this person is riding a different wave.
Could you not of even tried, not to sell; those white lies, which others gave?

Cannot control the weakness which governs, your fingertips to make the crime.
A heavy investment made, a deal gone wrong; messing with a lot of, precious time
A cheeky smile: the boys and girls, hide their frustrations from the ***Black shiny light.***
All madness tight fit in the jungle, ain't breaking into my soul; with such callous - ssshite.

Hot under the collar, sporting such flavors; so, unclean, degrading and raw.
Misinterpretations make 'Frontline News', injuring bones with an iron saw
Notorious such functions they bleed, but, the Horse's Mouth will always; be strait.
Calculating everything that needs to be readjusted, toothcombing with a kiwi slate

Can't erase what the papers say, as filthy ink has induced curious minds; to crawl and walk.
What of us, who have we become? As the reflexes keep on knocking; our opportunities to talk
Cannot save a witness from their own frivolous acts, where behavior appears quite; so, strange.
Indulged in victory we will achieve. For we ain't the ones smoking the crimson, leather change.

Battle Cries.

Military Procedures, all are suited and booted.
Fighting for our freedom, ones' fears; they were deep rooted
Rationed on food, for their families; they had to feed.
*A Crimson Red War, **Precious Blood;** scolds the people, as they bleed*

Lest we forget, what these remarkable people went through.
When will the sun set rise? To show us a day brand new.
The Sirens did sound, to the: 'Air Raid Shelters', they took.
Bombs away courage was needed, for the World indeed; it shook

Adrenaline rush from thinking, what's next will I ever know?
How will I ever be able, to dust off these raw emotions; in tow?
*Children crying, **First Aid** at hand; how has this all come to be?*
*Shops closing gone to War, the **Blackout's** Calling; it beckons thee.*

Houses ruined, fragile bones; sail to the other sides, bitter rage.
Historic moments which are now concealed, upon each precious page
See the plaques upon the wall shining brightly: Victorious indeed, to swallow.
And remember they gave their today, so that we may live to see; tomorrow

Why couldn't we just live in Peace? Instead of killing and waging War.
False Prophets gaining coins in riches, which were taken from; the poor
***'The Darkness'** chose each man and burnt each soul; to burden with pain.*
Now nothing can ever be how it was before, deeply saddened; never again

Step into a World so harrowing and experience their turmoil, right here today.
As these are the voices whose Ink imprinted, a phenomenal story; forever to stay
Depicting the decades in detail, these precious memories; can never be sold.
For the Battlefields mark great freedom, with the Medals of: 'Sunshine Gold'.

Spit & Rinse.

Dirty Bricks. Dirty Bricks.
Driven by the: Blood-Stained Pricks.
Dirty Bricks. ***Yes.*** *Dirty Bricks.*
Lacing bodies with ***bold,*** *green ticks.*

Skin and Bone. Skin and Bone.
Sucking the: 'Illuminous Ice-Cream Cone'.
Skin and Bone. ***Yes.*** *Skin and Bone.*
Electric-Sixes, Danger Zone.

Benefits for Rape. Benefits for Rape.
Who the hell decided, to skim this tape?
Benefits for Rape. ***Yes.*** *Benefits for Rape.*
Taken in and marked by: ***'Professor Snape'.***

Living Rough. Living Rough.
I have had, just about enough!
Living Rough. ***Yes.*** *Living Rough.*
Chasing Pavements, is extremely tough.

Laws that fail. ***Yes.*** *Laws that fail.*
Penning Conspiracies, sweet lies for sale.
Laws that fail. Laws that fail.
Punched like shots, by their: 'Holy Grail'.

Washing Machines, pipes and gongs.
Marching on with: ***'Protest Songs'.***
Brown paper bags and liberating banners.
All created to chalk, the greasy spanners.

Tight Curling tongs, in: 'Penguins' queue.
Mental Health sticks, to us like Glue.
Rocky Roads and sharp knitted suits.
Lured in by oppressions, seedy fruits.

'Pink Floyd' chisels, the eroded walls.
As we're placed upon, the glittered stalls.
Corbyn hangs, rustling up cakes; with the Kidz.
Plug this into Education's agenda, for Vids.

Theresa May, she's mucking about; with precious time.
It's all fancy footwork and expensive red wine.
Future Generations and 'Social Construction'.
Born into a smoke-filled world, of: Destruction.

Maple Syrup and spicy sounds.
Drink with wisdom. Avoid the Greyhounds.
Be a light. **Yes.** *Be a light.*
Flicker through, each stormy night.

Be a light. **Yes.** *Be a light.*
Don't go blind and lose your sight!!
Grab a hand and weave it with: Platinum Gold.
Don't fit in with what you've been, falsely told.

Donald Trump who has sure been tangoed, to death.
The hour is unknown, when we'll take our last breath.
Make Britain and America. Great again!
You avin' a laugh? We're back slashed by the cane.

Rewrite the pages, get your notebook and pens.
To change the distorted visual lens.
On a board of Whiskey, we are sliced skin deep.
Can I ask what's your Brand? You a Cow or a Sheep?

Injustice and venom dished out, by the: 'Talking Heads'.
Get in line, be good and down your meds.
Anti-Semitism, Misogyny and Racism; it's all up for grabs.
It makes juicy reading typed up, to exploit in the tabs.

The NHS is getting axed and it's slowly dying.
Mankind needs feeding, it's constantly crying.
Legs-It? Or Brexit? Place your bets at the bookies.
Sip your cold Coffee, chow down on your cookies.

Adult Social Services getting cut; whilst we rapidly bleed.
Chained to a Rhythm which drips, with ignorance and greed.
Assassinations and Reservations. All come at a cost!
For when War is promoted, you'll end up lost!

There's Guns and Knives and ISIS on our Pillars.
Dastardly dealings and Drip-Fed-Fred Killers.
It's a brown sugared rat-race, engraved in metal tins.
As we are all caked in powder and stamped with: 'Sick Sins'.

Tampon Tax invented, to fund Anti-Abortion.
Bloody Hell Man!! It's all out of proportion.
It's shocking and demoralizing, as we are all getting used.
Sucked in and chewed up, then spat out like a bruise.

Dot-to-Dot with the Russians. What filth do they swallow?
Who writes the Scripts?? And should we all follow?
Getting dragged on a plane, ripped apart at the seams.
Distorted Illusions and Elm Street Terror Dreams.

*Liquid COSHH breakfasts, dabbed in **hot blood.***
Chancin' with 'Marian' down in thick, sweaty mud.
Eating yellow chips, at the salty dock; foul mites.
***'The Hangman'** is calling, on your flesh; he bites.*

So, c'mon, tell me now. Please tell me now.
Can we ever beat, this: 'Crazy Cow'?
Yes. Tell me now. Please tell me now:
***Is the sweat still dripping, from your** Peachy Brow?*

General Poems

Black Dust.

'Oh' Lament it keeps on whispering
Through the tunnels, down below.
With each resounding blow

Children waking from sweet slumber.
Bleary eyed, they all must dread
*Footsteps in the **Black Dust,** they will have to tread.*

Eyes like a Panda: slowly coming up, to the shore
I bet your head is pounding, like a juicy apple core?
*For **Black** is the colour of Ill Health*

***Black** is the colour of the coal, in dust.*
*And **Black** remains the colour in which, our lungs; go bust*
***Black** is the colour of the clothes, they owned*

Imagine all the fatalities under-ground.
Imagine all the Fear by which, those children must be bound.
"We are the young children at work, down the mines,

opening and shutting the trap doors.
Who are we, that we should speak,
and who will fight our cause?".

"Oh, to play in daylight amongst others,
and feel the sun shining upon; our face.
We do but sit and wonder. Where is Love and Grace?".

Historical moments generations will remember
*For **Black** were the thoughts, of the children's call.*
*And **Black** are the memories prevailing; mining coal for all!*

McVitie's Disease.

Latch onto my Flesh.
Skin deep, injected Ink
Vessels burst, I sink.

In Crimson Waters, I swim
The stench, cuts me to the core.
Lost in translation; complications galore

In this place, you will have to stay.
Until the Persecutor chops down, your rustic chains
Electrical volts, piercing precious veins.

Like 'Denzil', I carry a 'Disease'
A 'Sandwich' of words spoken; Toxic Paradiddles.
Should I believe, these filthy riddles?

Asphyxiated; I cannot breathe.
For my Oxygen count, is severely low
*And this **Black Shadow,** just won't let go.*

Dislocated bones, no purpose served
Psychologically silent, unable to move.
Embedded nails, lay in the groove

Have you caught it yet? Na da.
Invisible, I did never exist
Hallucinations, added to the list!

Pitch Perfect? Hmm… Let me think.
Yes! Only if you're deluded, enough to swallow
The words of those Sheep, you continue to follow.

Gunshots fired; Blood trickles; feeling numb
It's dangerous, being inside your own head.
Excruciating pain, was it felt as you bled?

The Perpetrator, it was always you.
This Chilling Anthem, took maximum control
An Avenger in Battle, wreaking havoc to your soul.

True or False? Or insipid distortions? I ask.
Oppressed, are you? For wood chippings remain
Connections are yet to be, re-wired inside your brain.

Left only with a smidgen of belief.
As you have walked, Darth Vader's Road
Lay down your ashes and destroy; 'Da Vinci's Code'.

Surface Levels.

Censorious? Just quit it!
Assent... I do not need!
High Voltage won't make, me bleed

Pellucid? Well, that isn't me.
Introvert and deep, is my chosen style
Cold calculations, lay on your file.

Distinct from you, I am
Formerly tarnished and broken.
Trapped in time, a withheld token

The portal is enveloped in ***Darkness.***
The Grim Reaper, holds out His hand
Bam... In that place, I'm on remand.

A Mockingbird, you try to kill
With the gift, you've crafted so sweet.
Shaken and stirred... I'm off the beat!

Thunder bolted, a 'Fire Goblet' pawned.
Honeycomb transferred, the dices roll
Now in your hands, you take control.

Fantastical, trained thoughts; concealed
'Fagan's Generation'. Collects me or you?
Foul play not allowed; don't need a screw

This firm is heavy handed enough.
Loaded with Copper, Brass and Steel
My head, it's like a: 'Catherine Wheel'.

Such force, the sparks ignite
But to Grey, I will not fade.
For, I am an Ace; a Spade

Judgmental are you quitting? Hell no.
Approved? Who cares in my work, I am free.
A rare talent, was distributed to me!

Ambiguous? Cannot quite comprehend?
The queer points of view, I decided to bring
Precious Ink invested; designed to burn and sting.

Debt.

The age of the Card.
That left its mark.

That caused a fire.
A light, a spark.

Robotic People.
All in line.

Preying, prowling.
Recession time.

Fatal Cries.
And wounded souls.

The debtor's debt.
Leaves empty holes.

Addictions and Glamour.
Just put em', on Gold.

You will be crushed up
When their worth, does unfold.

Tormented, chained up.
You beckoned, at its call.

Ashamed, instilled with fear.
For you've hit a Brick Wall.

A generation rising.
All greed, no thinking.

The era that left.
Each person sinking.

So, consumed by quicksand.
Overridden, weighed down.

Temptations took hold:
In this, a: 'Ghost Town'.

The Wooden Witch.

Disheveled and eerie looking.
Life like in a form, so rare
She resides in, spacious woodlands.
She gives out, a deadly stare

To the eye, so creepy and gaunt.
Sending chills, right down your spine
A season of: ***Darkness*** *prevailing.*
Associations with: 'Frankenstein'.

Hunched over in, the cemented ground.
Captivating passers-by, each day
'The Wooden Witch', has made her mark.
She is, a Predator; enticing her Prey

Scraggly hair resting upon, her shoulders.
'A Sorting Hat', to decide ones' fate
A Battle between Good and Evil.
'Gryffindor' only; can make her truly great

Hands so crooked, like: 'Fagan's Flock'.
Chipped and tarnished, in full view
Slowly dissolving beneath, the cracks.
Of the dry land that is broken, in two

Cheek bones, that are well defined.
A grumpy expression, a sour face
One Witch standing silent, unnerving.
'Black Shadows' *consume, her designated space*

Eyes emotionless, dead as the night.
***Jet Black** pupils, that lure you in*
A sculpture magnificently crafted.
Impressions wedged deep under, your skin

Green Moss covers her Ghostly Silhouette.
Withered and frail, ever she will be
'Voldemort's Accomplice' keeps on calling:
"The woods are where you must, join me".

The Library Ladies.

We met at the Library, 'Geek C'est Chic'.
November 2015, crossing paths; entwined
Amongst book lovers, writers and fellow poets.
A new relationship indeed, was aligned

I was intrigued, when I scanned the room.
Never thought 'Maid Marian', would be a friend
Encouraging, quirky and passionate.
Coming on board, so we could start; a new trend

I've got the nerdy glasses; my look sure fits the bill.
She's got the ideas, to catch ones' eye
In unison comparing, our thoughts and views.
Lifting our voices, so they do not run dry

*Gimme an **F**, we indeed make it Fun.*
*Gimme a **G**, let's strike some new Chords*
*Gimme a **B**, yes plenty of Books.*
'Harry Potting' our: 'Magic Swords'.

*Gimme a **C**, full of Character; we are.*
Gimme two A's, Gold Stars; for us
*Gimme an **E**, full of Edge; that's right.*
*Gimme a **H**, so sharp; 'Hot Fuzz'.*

These Library Ladies, have sure learnt the lingo.
How to craft masterpieces so sweet, in tune
No Red Buzzers visible, on the: 'A-Teams' table.
For, rare talent only lays within, this room

*Giving a **T**, our vocabulary is Teaching.*
*Giving a **P**, moral support we Provide*
*Giving a **D**, we are Driven to succeeding.*
As we both share, one another's journey; in tide

*We were given an **O**, for Opportunity.*
*We were given an **M**, to make our Mark*
*We were given an **L**, to climb the Ladder.*
Instant Coffee bonding, to create a spark

*We added an **R**, Raw gift to the mix.*
*Capital **K**, as we Knelt exposed*
Open and vulnerable in view.
Not knowing what would be, proposed

So, you see, we are both clued up to the max.
Lyrically firing, Double L's; Blazin' Squad.
For, it is in the Library that month; that we met
Once strangers, now acquainted; how very odd!

Chicken Run.

Like. Like. Like.
This is what's wrong with the world.
Love. Love. Love.
Knitted into Technology's hand glove.
Conversations in Stones, are rolling
Knee boots: continue strolling.
Out of control, on this highway
Exploited by its sticky foreplay.
Fingertips glued to a glass, induced screen
Rattling bones and tearing up your spleen.
Mashed Potato, in: 'Skeletors Queue'.
Polishing its exterior to me, to you.
Chuckling hardcore, can you see the blood?
Laced where we stand, around puddles of Mud.
Like. Like. Like.
High rise transmitters of: Graphic Porn.
Love. Love. Love.
Sink your teeth into the seedy, cobbled corn.
Superglued and deeply addicted
Interests in gold, greatly conflicted.
Gone are the days, of face-to-face talk
It's a generation dusted, in powdered chalk.
Must. Must. Must.
Got to have all the latest top-notch trends
Otherwise you choke, on the metal bends.
Use. Use. Use.
Facebook, Twitter, Google and more
Sucked in and bitten, right down to the core.
Take. Take. Take.

A slab, a drag, a taxi, a cab, a bus, a car, a plane,
a lift, the stairs; high fevered in flares.
A day, a minute, an hour, a second, a life, a heart;
a tongue. A bittersweet melody, always sung.
We remain Pied Piping to a: 'Glittered Gun'.
Distorted like Chickens', in a: Honey Glazed Run.

Some Days.

Some Days: I just can't cope, pass me a knife
*So, I can skim the pages in **blood;** talking life.*
Shaky hands write, as my clothes they do fall
Tearing flesh scraped by a razor, bricked wall.
Silhouettes dance in dust, pain hangs me dry
Exposing my naked bones, so you see me cry.
Dignity. Gone! I've been laced in: 'Sweet Rum'.
And rolled into the barrel, of a loaded Gun.
Some Days: I'm weak, I'm tired and feel sick
*As I'm smoked **dark green,** by a fat; juicy tick.*
Like a slave in the wild, battered and bruised
I'm like cheesy grub, never left; always used.
Apple Trees shrivel and my tongue, it beats
Knitted tightly like skirts, with folded pleats.
Some Days: I'm jealous, I'm angry; I'm lost
Overthinking in Scarlett, to predict the cost.
Laced in boiling water, trying not to explode
Some Days it's carnage, on: 'Damascus Road'.
Chasing Skittles to realign, the days of worry
Penning mustard rhymes, like: Vindaloo Curry.

Electric Heat.

Go shred it like meat, on a peppered bone.
And then bathe it in silk, to fiercely touch
Free running from the lips, salty; yet tasty.
As Caramel in Honey, Combs your Crutch
Glitter Bomb the streets with, Mint products.
*Unleash the tongues to talk **bold,** never greed*
Grab the withered hands whose ink, did scorn.
*Rewinding, **Mr. Raspberry's** potential; to bleed*
Fizzled frenzies, should ignite bones; to welcome.
Opening veins to ooze sweet blood, creating fire
Drenched in paper cuts, as we sweat fine feathers.
To dance, the other side of the: 'Holocaust's Wire'.
Kaleidoscope exotic progression, throughout life
Because with White nibs, we can crystallize scars.
Electrifying flesh with static heat, that distributes:
'Yellow Pills, A Class'; which drive us to echo: Mars.

Flashbacks.

Lost your mind?
But followed your heart.
Where do you start?

The memories, a token.
The years, passed by
Silent tears, do you cry?

What are you to think?
What are you to do?
With pierced words, gone through.

Tampering with emotions?
Dark thoughts in your head?
Bearing the pain, for you bled.

Camouflage Patterns.
Hidden in the background
Drained out by the sound.

Broken in two
Questions flow through your mind.
About the way, you were designed

*You scream in **bright blood***
Saying: "I cannot stop being me".
For others hold the chains, you see.

In a glass house
People shouldn't through stones.
But rather, watch their overtones

Sensory overload.
Electricity, shooting through your veins
Are you scarred, by what remains?

History, do not repeat.
What has already been done
You are, which one?

A tormented soul, are you?
Mixed up deep down, inside
How did you find this ride?

Boomtown Ratz.

The Fireworks, have just sounded.
The Vagabonds, come quickly running.

Lip-Sticking Treacle, for: 'Tiffany'.
*The **'Dark Arts'**, how very cunning.*

Slits... On their precious wrists.
For, lost generations; they do but, bleed.

*Eating **P!nk Salmon,** at Vera's House.*
#Hash Tagging: "Afromanned on Tumbleweed".

The Rookies, what a clown.
Bacon Butties, that's their style.

Watching all the 'Metal Heads'.
***Red-Boxing** 'Nickelback', on speed dial.*

This Plague like picture, I am painting.
Is catastrophic, breaks down your door.

For, dead bodies lace; the streets at night.
Soaked in needles, glued to: 'Pinheads Claw'.

Trainspotters, three wheelin' our estates.
With Sex and Violence, ever wild.

Plastered on our screens, frontline:
"We'll style your Council, Child!".

Smarties drizzle, those hungry mouths.
As people watch their Platinum Clocks.

"I need my fix of: Champagne Sugar".
Cough up payment!! Here's my socks.

Letters come alive, they skim the walls.
With steely tongues, they do; but ***RIOT!***

This is: 'England' at its; 'Georgy Best'.
Killing you, with its: Filthy Brown Bread, Diet.

Tight Shrinks, dressed in 'Straitjackets'.
Staple Squirrels, to their spoken rails:

"Nutty Patients, we've no beds left dears,
just, these icy corridors hard as nails".

Ebeneezer quaffs, as I stand speaking:
"This is destruction, it craves; no rest.

I want to walk in shoes, you've branded.
And take your venom, out of their chest".

They'll smoke your pockets, like sketch.
They'll sell their soul, to fund their habit.

They'll dance with the 'Devil Incarnate'.
Shooting, tiny veins like: 'Roger Rabbit'.

Even the Cuckoo's have needs; they pray.
And we must listen, to their beady cries.

For, what good are we; if we ignore?
Their existence and worth, with blissful sighs.

So, when the snappers sound outside.
Whether it's a myth or truth, to bare.

Remember, this poet who came to: 'Sheeptown'.
To beg you, not to: ***Demonize*** *Kidz, in Care.*

Lying Eyes.

2008 shocked the Nation, with Corruption
Friendships were tested and sparks were flying.
A little girl, so tender; just nine years' old
Chained in an Asylum. A case too horrifying.

Abandoned Love, just plain greed and slaughter
Towards a precious soul, her own baby daughter.
Solidarity from a Community, oblivious to lies
For, in one mixed up house; whispered silent cries.

There was disbelief in the mind of me; the watcher
"Very soon you'll be busted. I hope they clock ya".
Suspicions and Behaviours, they sparked concern
The pushing of boundaries, made my stomach churn.

Deep hatred on the rise, wanting truth to unfold
As one callous parent, cheats the System for: Gold!
It's hard to flip the coin, to see a different view
And to believe that such a tale, was ever true.

Hungry mouths and Monopoly, started to dictate
With Controversial Affairs spread wide, in debate.
Loud cheers sound, as the Balloons reach the sky
Educationally subnormal? Designed to sting and lie?

From Council Estates, branded common as muck
And sticky labeled as idle, not giving one fuck.
Are children just property for a game, in time?
Penned venomously without thought, for crime?

I am left feeling melancholic and raw to the bone
Should **'The Hangman'**, *have marked; their zone?*
I cannot believe what I have witnessed, it's insane
Carnage claiming the innocent, bruising with pain.

Anonymity for the mother, to meet her Human Rights.
Raiding Taxpayers' Pockets, to fund her new delights.
She's now unable to get a job, for what she has done
And, if that were me; I'd spend my life on the run.

But, what of Shannon; where is she this very day?
What's her story and what would she have to say?
Never forgotten is this historical event, on stage
And never forgotten are the lions, in the cage.

But, listeners please be aware; that sanity, it falls
*For, life ain't always easy; beyond these **Red** walls.*
I'm not condoning what she did, but you see
Maybe, she was just a little damaged: 'Oak Tree'.

Gathering tea cups from the storm, that was looming
It leaves questions beneath the wires, that were grooming.
So, let us remember the twisted fingertips; that fell
Down on our papers leaving, a bittersweet; pungent smell!

The Gingerbread Man.

{Dedicated to the host of: 'The Writers Bookshelf'}.
Drystone Radio, Cowling, North Yorkshire.

He's like pepper, laced in candy
Smoking Hot, his polish runs.
Down your throat, so sweetly
For, he doesn't dish out guns.

He's like glitter, in your pocket
Chalking veins with juices; sweet.
Dancing in your bloodstream
Fires crackin', burning heat.

Keith Lemon. Doppelganger.
Through the Keyhole, on his show.
With zest and spark; mint humour
Introduced to make, you glow.

Handing out the medicine bottle
Creating vibes, to paint a smile.
He's like Sunshine, in the Rain
'Gingerlicious Infections', of style.

He's like Cucumber, ever cool
Whiskey drizzled, on the rocks.
Yes, David that's my Driver:
Always kind. He never mocks.

Invisible Chains.

Do you see the Scissors, in my tired eyes?
Or the slits on my wrists, which bleed?
Do you see the maps, smothered in steel?
***Blackberries** hold me, on a metal lead.*

Does my face resemble, tenebrous letters?
*For I am stained, with the: **'Devil's Dust'**.*
As my bones freeze, locked up in pain
Gnawing down on a mouldy, bread crust.

Do you see the flesh dissolving, rapidly?
As the Crows peck away, at your insides.
A Victim at 'Shutter Islands', Bleak Gate.
As Cherries, Smoke you; like stygian tides.

No dancing with Velvet, beneath the stars
For Body Rockers, like Skeletons'; crawl.
Through your veins, to torment your soul
Whispering: "We come to make you fall".

Different perceptions, drip feeding ears
But, what of me - Who Am I? ACHOO!
Just another statistic, on paper to chase?
Medicated, in: 'Striped Pyjamas' queue?

Am I a ghost for my plasters, are hidden?
Where is Mr. Mango, to hold my hand?
*You ask, drenched in: **Noirs** Salt-Bath.*
As 'Hamlet' divides, this previous land.

Abusive fingertips, that pocket shrapnel.
Those streets I roamed, are empty tombs
For the 'Army Kids', are on their way.
Boxing Crackers, into ***darkened*** *rooms.*

Can ignorance be sliced, razor sharp?
Let's eradicate oppression, here, today.
Cleansing souls injected, with dynamite:
'To knock 'Bellatrix', right out of our way'.

<u>Her Name is Claire.</u>

{Dedicated to No: 10 Coffee House, Haworth}.

When the shops fall silent.
And faces look down, at the empty floor
With negative attitudes prevailing.
Rustic and barren is the land, once more

Where are the pleasant exchanges?
The golden smiles, to spread the light?
Customer Service, so hard to find
Highly Professional, 5-star; polite.

Drab and dreary people, around the circumference.
Bolshie and brazen, unapproachable for sure
Time indeed it is, so precious.
But, to provide help for some; is a major chore

Gone are the days, of extreme effort.
Gone are the days, of welcoming hands
And gone are the days, of professional triumph.
No witness boxes, just hollow sheep; vicious rams.

Services which lack, the Burning Sun.
But beware, Sweet Melodies; are near
Get up to Haworth, to Number: ***10.***
Deeply satisfying is the service here

Remember, her name is Claire.
Above others, who failed to show
Customer Service at its very best.
Ill Standards, she does not know.

Take a moment to capture, the madness
The mannerisms which let, your experience down.
And remember that place, made known to you
Up yonder, less chaotic; out of town.

I cannot yet quite fully, comprehend.
These cities which use, foul play
Shopping that once was so enjoyable.
Now spoilt by those: ***Jars of Clay.***

Customer Service so solid, once gone
But not when Claire, is on the block.
For, her presence is gentle and impeccably kind
Crystallized, like that of a: Precious Rock.

'Happy Valley', is not always guaranteed.
For services unpredictable, will ever be
But, I remembered this one amazing lady.
Whose quaint little shop, was so comforting to me

So, remember her name is Claire.
And her skills, score high above the rest
For, when the land is silent and barren.
Let Number: ***10,*** *pierce your weary chest!*

Best Friends?

Do you have a Best Friend?
Have you loved? Have you shared?
Have you lost? Have you cared?
Has it ever, come to an end?
Fighting talk, abstruse conversations?
Defensive attitudes and mixed interpretations?
Arrogance, ignorance and neglect?
Do you ever tend, to reflect?
On the feelings of one another.
Those times of help, when both were short
Even though the times prevailing.
Left you burdened and things still fraught
Why did all this, come to be?
Life throws sticky moments, your way.
But, do you turn; your backs?
Or keep the strength and stay?
It certainly takes two, to tango
How very true, that's right you are.
But remember this one, important thing:
You'll always jump back, on the bonnet of the car.
Time, it is a great healer
Although some friendships, ain't meant to be.
But, you guys just keep on smiling
And let happiness set, you free.
So, do you have a Best Friend?
Have you failed? Have you persevered?
Were bank accounts, sufficiently cleared?
This page is yours, to map out the end.

Don't live there; live here.

Don't live there, live here; for it will only burden, your soul.
Don't live there, live here; it will fill your cup and make, you whole
Don't live there I say; for there is only **'Darkness'**, *in a cloudy mind.*
Don't live there, live here; a much better place, so placid and kind

Don't live there, live here; for you're never going back, to troubled times.
Don't live there, live here; and bust out some fresh, new lyrical rhymes
Don't live there, live here; a much more solid and healthier place.
Don't live there, live here; adjusting, pressing on with the race

Don't live there, live here; for, it is filled with Sunshine and positive vibes.
Don't live there, live here; in the present day, surfing the: 'Strangest of Tides'.
Don't live there, live here; for you cannot change, what has already been done.
Don't live there, live here; in the Light hanging out, beneath the Blazing Sun

Don't live there, live here; where this Valley offers new opportunities, indeed for all.
Don't live there, live here; no looking back at the **Shadows,** *which made; you fall*
Don't live there, live here; embracing each day that was given, as a new lifeline.
Don't live there, live here; let not the past claim, your Golden hours in precious time

Don't live there, live here; in the place where Living Waters, are sure to flow.
Don't live there, live here; train your mindset, to think positive and let go
So, don't live there, live here; where you can be sure, that things will change.
Don't live there, live here; and kiss goodbye to that Butcher: **'Steve so Strange'**.

Chicken Coop Range.

Blood, Blood. Everywhere
Stripped dead bare
Without a care.
Blood, Blood. Everywhere
Stripped dead bare
All stop to stare.
Keep the Jester, far away
And please send Kester, right my way.
To hold my hand and guide me home
To that place where I, can weep alone.
Distorted Illusions.
And Sugar Coated Confusions.
*Lost to **'Parklifes'**, edgy tune.*
"Cheerio, we'll be back soon".
Drip-Fed-Fred
Climbs into my bed.
To melt my head
See where I bled.
Skin and Bone.
Cut down to the core.
Just leave me here
*At **deaths,** glamorous door.*
Can't take the heat
For, my scars; they show.
But, what now for me?
Who will want to know?
About my Demons?
My darkness and pain?
The bittersweet melodies.
*Of a body: **'INSANE'.***
Magicians strike me, in waters cold
As I am welded into, the frosty mould.
'Skeletor' mocks, as he's passing by
For salty tears you do, but cry.
Haunted by the 'Silver Mesh':
***'Black** cannot ever change'.*
The Cherry Kisses, that marked:
You down at: 'Coopers Chicken Range'.

Life is: Diabolical!

Life is: Diabolical! It smokes you, with Cherries and Leather
And burns your eyes like Dynamite, in the seas of: Stormy Weather.
It misjudges and plays Monopoly, with your mind; wrapped in, its maze
And takes you down to 'Georgia', to dance: 'The Peanut Buttered Craze'.

It exploits your: Human Rights, dabs them; in Vinegar and bloody Salt
Whilst playing ping-pong with your emotions, as fast as: Usain Bolt.
It traffics you to lick, crepitate candy from the gutter
Laced in Peachy Juices, as you man its seedy shutter.

It separates joint communities, crushes dreams and deals in hate
I'm standing here sweating diamond tears, as I pen, with chalk; your slate.
It manipulates and sells you lies, like puppets on a string
And politically plots the races with a ***Fascist,*** *who is out to* ***WIN!***

It bleeds your pockets dead dry, to rebuild the: 'First Class Crystal Palace'
Yes, my darlings welcome, to this town called: 'Fucking Malice'.
It treats you like 'Magic Dust', you're nothing: you don't matter
For, your bones are piled high on my skip, because with glass; I come to shatter.

It sucks you off like sex, gagging, for cut-throat; sonic times
Why are we chained and suffocated, by its filthy worded crimes?
Thatcher's risen from the dead and ***'Scatman',*** *well he's just barking mad*
This life is: Diabolical! I think, 'Hitler's Breaking Nations - Bad'.

Gas Lighter.

She Gaslights, she's devious.
Manipulates to make it, his fault
Traps him in her stained, glass vault.

She Gaslights sadly, it's his sanity; he's losing
Incapacitated Distortions. With severe bruising.

Hot flames wax the crooked candles, as they rock
***Animalistic Fears** netted in tights, down on the dock.*

*Bitten hard, the **Scarlett blood;** fiercely explodes upstairs*
For, there's beauty in the realms of: Psychotic Snares.

Poppin' the magic pills to make him: 'Limp Bizkit'; Numb
Washed like a machine chewing, Bubble Flavoured Gum.

She Gaslights, her 'Rookie Blue' eyes; they don't leak
Spinning Cobwebs making, her husband dead weak.

Bittersweet licks mark these pages, with Marmite paste
She's blinded in vision, he's dog collared to; her waist.

She Gaslights, he flickers; knitted tightly at the seams
For, Fairy Liquid dissolves; all his hopes and dreams.

Power imbalances, they lead to 'Inequality Streets'
Frying people like eggs, hissing; 'Punk Toned Beats'.

He's down on his luck, he can't take it anymore
I wish he'd just leave her and walk out of that door.

But, it's not that simple, for the 'Sum of 41'; is too deep
Not brazen like cattle. He's 'Shaun the Woolly Sheep'.

We might not be close, but he's still flesh and bone
And I don't like to think of him, in this danger zone.

***Intense Darkness** rising and Destabilising thoughts*
A Tennis ball for a head, smashed; upon the courts.

A 'Victim of Love' in a hypnotic trance and a daze
He's like a 'Goblet of Fire', in a smoke-filled maze.

Without his Weetabix, he's cabbaged; he can't think
For he's 'Mashed like Potato'; bottled up to drink.

On an old rugged chess board, his heart; is her slave
His 'Abuser' she dances: on his rosy thorn, grave.

'The Tasmanian Devil' strikes her spell, one way
Candy Flossing his brain, until his: 'Teeth Decay'.

18094088R00043

Printed in Poland
by Amazon Fulfillment
Poland Sp. z o.o., Wrocław